RICHARD SERRA DRAWINGS

CELEBRATING

ORDOVAS

2011 — 2021

In 2012 my friend John Silberman asked if I could help to find an institutional venue in the UK or Europe for Richard Serra to show his latest drawings: ideally, he wanted an intimate space and of course the sooner, the better. In October 2013 the *Courtauld Transparencies* were shown at the The Courtauld Gallery.

It was a privilege to be able to help make that exhibition a reality and, in the process, get to spend time with Richard and Clara Serra. In February 2013 we visited The Courtauld together. I have always found it revealing and exciting to look at art through the eyes of an artist, and seeing some of Richard's favourite Cézanne paintings, and the Prints and Drawings Study Room – I remember specially the late Michelangelo drawing of Christ on the cross – are experiences I will never forget.

It was also wonderful to see Richard and Clara looking at the space at The Courtauld and getting enthused and thinking of the exhibition together. Later, at lunch in Wilton's, I was fascinated to see how Serra would use his sketch book to show us works he was referring to, or spaces … his thoughts articulated in drawings.

There are nineteen works presented in our exhibition, selected by Serra. Orchard Street refers to the street where the artist and Clara have a home on the North Fork of Long Island. Serra has his drawing studio there and it is there that they currently spend most of their time. To be able to show the *Orchard Street* series of drawings at our gallery is a dream come true and I would like to thank John, Trina, Clara and above all Richard for making this exhibition a reality.

Drawing is always an indication of how artists think. [...] Drawing defines how one collects material through scale, placement and edge.

—RICHARD SERRA

Richard Serra, *Blank*, 1978, Stedelijk Museum, Amsterdam

I think people have
largely lost their sense of touch.

—RICHARD SERRA

As a child, Richard Serra came to terms with the world the way most of us do: he converted the facts around him into a private, tactile experience in which the act was as significant as the end result. He has recounted how he would draw on rolls of pink paper that his mother obtained from a friendly butcher in San Francisco, sometimes analysing the parts of an engine that his father and brother were trying to rebuild.[1] Drawing earned Serra a place at Yale for postgraduate study in fine art, and has remained as central throughout his career as the sculptural achievements for which he is best known. If anything, drawing is the dominant paradigm in Serra's understanding of art. 'I read almost all art through drawing', he said in 1992. 'Drawing is always an indication of how artists think. […] Drawing defines how one collects material through scale, placement and edge.'[2]

Drawing can be as nascent as the ideas that Serra records in the notebooks he keeps close to hand, or as emphatic as the walls of a room. Some of his works are site-specific, or at least site-conditioning: they operate in conjunction with interior spaces to affect viewers' experiences of those spaces (p. 5). The results accentuate one's sense of being present in relation to spaces that, once adjusted, become somehow explicit in the mind. These large-scale drawings expand the basic elements of graphic expression to the point where they test the definitions and boundaries of the medium. Comparable challenges characterise Serra's approach to all the media with which he has engaged since the mid-1960s. Other drawings, such as *Nova Scotia I*, 1983, (p. 9) record direct, intimate impressions of his large-scale sculptural projects – in this case, *Clara-Clara*, 1983. Drawing allows Serra to come to terms with his own sculptures by realising his impressions in graphic form.

Since the 1990s, Serra has also developed a fecund set of techniques for another category of drawings. The results constitute a sizeable body of work that includes the *Orchard Street* series, 2018, and this kind of drawing embodies a sense of relations noticeably different from that found in his earlier large-scale interventions. The earlier works are by their nature communal opportunities for individualised kinetic experience. The *Orchard Street* drawings are smaller, intimate, and not predicated upon a specific location. They are noticeably more private works that Serra produced in his studio without assistance, and intended as self-contained objects that require a viewer, light, and a modicum of space. If this approach seems like a domestication of Serra's practice, there is little familiar about the tactile vocabulary involved. The results differ markedly not only from his other types of drawing, but also from anything else in the history of drawing as a medium.

Richard Serra, *Nova Scotia I*, 1983

The general process that Serra uses to make this kind of drawing involves a viscous medium spread upon a horizontal surface, heavy sheets of handmade paper laid atop, and a set of metal weights that Serra uses as tools to press the paper onto the medium, adjusting them in his hand to control the degree and concentration of pressure. Sometimes, though not in the *Orchard Street* drawings, he uses intermediaries such as wire mesh to constrain his material. His primary medium over the years has been molten paintstick, although in recent series he has added or substituted other substances that produce noticeably different effects. Perhaps the most significant feature of these drawings is that they involve a transfer process: Serra works on the verso of each sheet until he intuits when he should stop. He then lifts the paper from the viscous material, which often collects in peaks and clusters that give these drawings their distinctively topographic surfaces. The results always contain an element of surprise, for Serra cannot know how each drawing will come out until he lifts the sheet and pins it to the studio wall. In that respect, the conventional temporal flow of drawing – the present-tense gathering of coherence, immediately apparent and adjustable – is disrupted and displaced.

The *Orchard Street* drawings followed directly from the *Rotterdam Verticals* series, 2016-17, (pp. 14-15) that Serra produced for an exhibition at the Museum Boijmans Van Beuningen, Rotterdam, in 2017. The two series have in common a material that Serra has favoured in recent series of drawings, a blend of etching ink and silica. That material, unlike paintstick, requires no heating. It is more fluid and the high pigment load in etching ink allows extremely dense, rich blacks. In addition to its effect on the texture of the vehicle, silica also adds light-diffusing and brightening properties. The *Rotterdam Verticals* and *Orchard Street* drawings share a structural predicate – the term 'composition' seems misplaced in discussions of Serra's work, although within the logic of drawing as a discipline it is valid – of arrayed vertical strokes that collect varying quantities of black matter on the recto of each drawing. The lean accumulations of *Orchard Street #75*, for example, reveal the underlying equipoise of decisive gesture and intuitive arrangement that characterises Serra's technique. Each stroke along the paper is individually assertive without implying a contingent relationship with another stroke; no modelling occurs, no described contours or shading that might imply a narrative legibility. The marks are structural but not crucial, interrelated but not interdependent.

Although this pared-down graphic sensibility is recognisably within historical conventions of drawing, the material that adheres to the paper strays towards the point where we might legitimately wonder how elastic those conventions really are.

One answer lies in the structural constancy of the series as a whole. The linear accumulations of *Orchard Street #75* or even *#82*, two of the more heavily worked drawings in the series, are no less apparent for the bituminous surfaces that elide the underlying vertical strokes. At heart, drawing is a medium that depends upon the transformation of manual action into lines that develop over time and remain evident after the action has ceased. Implicit in this notion is all of the present-tense action – drawing as pulling, drawing as part of our language for kinetic forces within and beyond fine art – that contributes to our commonsensical understanding of drawing as physically immediate. We do not readily think of drawing as an indirect, or even rehearsed or repeated, mode of artistic expression.

This leads us to an inherent discrepancy in Serra's drawings: an intriguing misalignment between the traits of the medium as Serra uses it and the linguistic uncertainty that results. Even if we ignore the rhetoric that coalesces around Serra and his practices – the industrial, Vulcanian motifs that come too easily to mind – it is difficult to reconcile the language of graphic finesse with the physical facts of the *Orchard Street* drawings. There is no appropriate term in drawing for the clusters of material that pucker and bubble into surfaces for which the vocabulary of painting (impasto, for example) is also inaccurate. The behaviour of material ultimately decides the language appropriate to it. Neither ink nor paintstick, however, is usually expected to behave in the ways that Serra has developed and refined. His graphic materials sometimes take on the aura of heavy industry, not least when they are physically conditioned by analogous forces. In truth, there are also plenty of industrial processes involved in conventional approaches to drawing today. Ink slurry is milled, for example, and pencils do not manufacture themselves. The difference is that Serra's techniques imply those processes in unprecedented proximity to the moment of execution. This is a particular kind of immediacy that conventionally attends other media, but seldom drawing. There is nothing, however, that countermands its validity as a graphic strategy.

A similar kind of immediacy quickened Serra's early forays into what became a renowned sculptural practice. Perhaps the purest example is *To Lift*, 1967, (p. 13) an astonishingly straightforward exemplification not only of sculptural precepts, but also of Serra's observation that 'drawing defines how one collects material'. A rectilinear sheet of rubber becomes volumetric and curvilinear when it is drawn upwards. It finds acceptable moments of equipoise that allow those dynamic forces to persist in states of arrest. As with *To Lift*, so with the ink-and-silica blend that acts of drawing convert into variegated clusters as Serra lifts the paper from the horizontal plane. The nineteen examples from the *Orchard Street* series that appear here collect material according to a relatively constrained set of manual

Richard Serra, *To Lift*, 1967, The Museum of Modern Art, New York

Richard Serra, *Rotterdam Vertical #3*, 2017

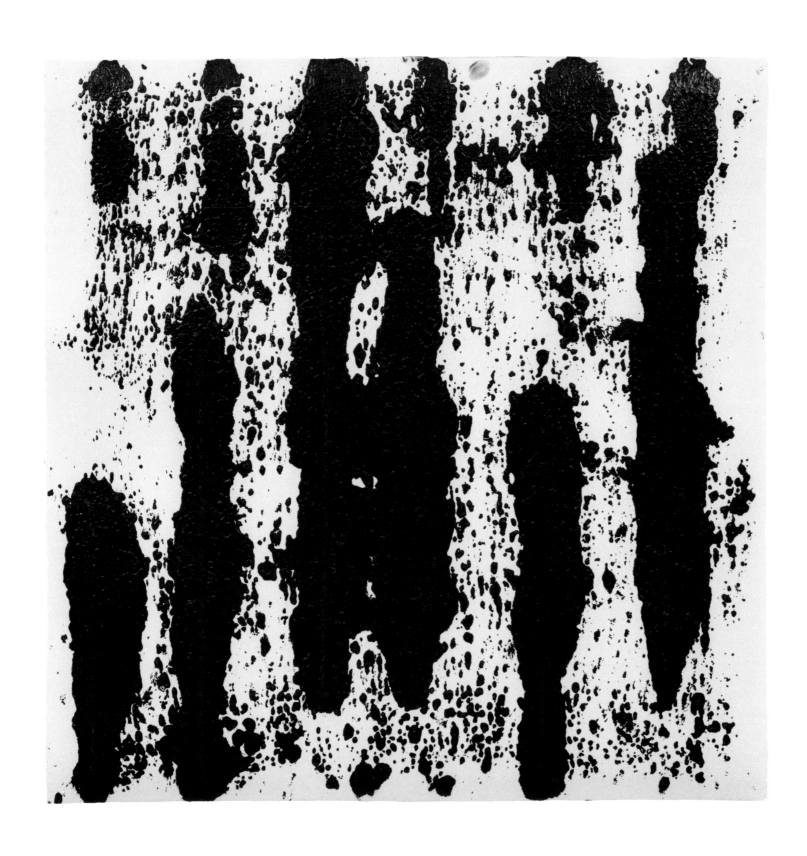

Richard Serra, *Rotterdam Vertical #9*, 2017

operations, but the resulting effects are ultimately physical facts in states of equilibrium rather than devices of aesthetic persuasion. They do not attempt to tell us anything beyond, if one wishes to enquire, how they came to be.

In *Orchard Street #90*, for example, the flat black imposed field also forms a ground for the granulated texture of ink and silica where friction and shear forces have conspired to record a compressed sequence of straightforward actions. The same material, manual handling and forces might be combined in any number of drawings without replicating this specific result, or the specific result of any other drawing. The non-repeatability of drawing is particularly important for Serra: 'I think my whole drawing practice is involved with repetition, knowing there's no possibility of repeating, knowing that it's going to yield something different every time.'[3] In *The Shape of Time*, a book that proved important for Serra and other artists of his generation, the art historian George Kubler observed that 'a symbol exists by virtue of repetitions'.[4] Serra's suspicion of representation and narrative is connected to their distancing effects as interpretations of material facts. 'I'm not involved with narrative', he told Hal Foster during a conversation about figuration. 'If you're involved with narrative, you're involved with the language of narration and representation as well as imagery, and that overrides form – it diverts from the experience of form.'[5] Symbols, like any other conversion of material facts into language, intercede between the viewer and the object in ways that Serra's aesthetic choices strive to make experientially redundant.

Instead of expressive symbols, or the connotations that flow from graphic conventions in figuration, Serra deploys the elements of drawing without the implications of legible assembly. The feathering and smearing in *Orchard Street #98*, or the interplay of reflected and absorbed light in *#71*, are direct results of physical processes and properties. They do not signify anything specific – there is no story or metaphysical implication towards which they point – but they nonetheless invoke an existing vocabulary of pictorial subtlety. Habits are stubborn, and so the open, loosely contoured tonal characteristics that invigorate frozen moments might still suggest the possibility of an interpretive whole, as though meaning might somehow emerge if the viewer is diligent or patient enough. This is one understanding of meaning: meaning as a container that might be malleable or permeable, but is nonetheless at least provisionally closed. In Serra's drawings, as in so many innovations that have guided advanced art since the 1940s, meaning is better understood not as something works of art possess, but as something they do. This is 'meaning' not as noun but as gerund; in process, unfixed.

This is one reason why disciplinary contours are important in Serra's creative practices, why the distinctions among them remain valid and even reinforced despite apparent challenges to them. There are obviously aspects of these drawings that are comparable to printmaking. Indeed, Serra's approach to printmaking also expands that discipline: he applied paintstick to screenprints in *Robeson*, 1985, for example, and introduced silica to create a grainy physical depth in the *Reversal* series, 2015 (p. 19). The transfer technique of the *Orchard Street* drawings and their kin veers towards the physical relations of printmaking, as does the pivotal moment of lifting the paper from the mark-making medium. The most important differences are temporal. Tense and aspect – when something happens, how long it takes, whether or not it is completed – become defining characteristics. A print is a realised instance taken from a preexisting configuration of ink or something similar. It has, in effect, two separate episodes of perfect-tense completion: one when the design is finalised, another when the print has been taken. A drawing, on the other hand, is an evolution *ex nihilo* of marks directly onto the support. The marks of a print are, with few exceptions (such as Serra's own), translated indices of things that have already happened. The marks in a drawing are preserved indices of things that are happening.

If this seems to be an excessively refined distinction, it nonetheless recapitulates in microcosm a significant feature of art-historical development. One of the better-known anecdotes from the Renaissance is Giotto's circle. According to Vasari, a Papal envoy sought evidence of skill from notable painters. Instead of a finished drawing, Giotto drew a perfect circle without tools of geometry.[6] Ernst Gombrich contrasted this notion of perfect draughtsmanship with Leonardo's approach two hundred years later, giving as an example the studies for the Virgin and Child with St Anne and the Infant Baptist, *circa* 1505-08 (pp. 20-21). Leonardo made so many adjustments and alterations to his composition that much of it is almost illegible. He ultimately traced his preferred arrangement on the verso with a stylus. Leonardo, unlike most of his contemporaries, did not treat drawing as a quest for conclusion and stasis – the perfect form, with imperfection eliminated – but rather as an heuristic animation of form. Leonardo, Gombrich wrote, 'works like a sculptor modelling in clay who never accepts any form as final but goes on creating, even at the risk of obscuring his original intentions.'[7] The goal is not perfection, but rather the vividly imperfect characteristics of change over time.

This is a precarious, and untidy, way to work. There is no particular sense of an ideal, no *O di Giotto* to serve as a paragon of execution or as an aesthetic objective to be emulated. Serra's approach has more in common with Leonardo's practice of variable recapitulation, which is very different from repetition.

Richard Serra, *Reversal I*, 2015

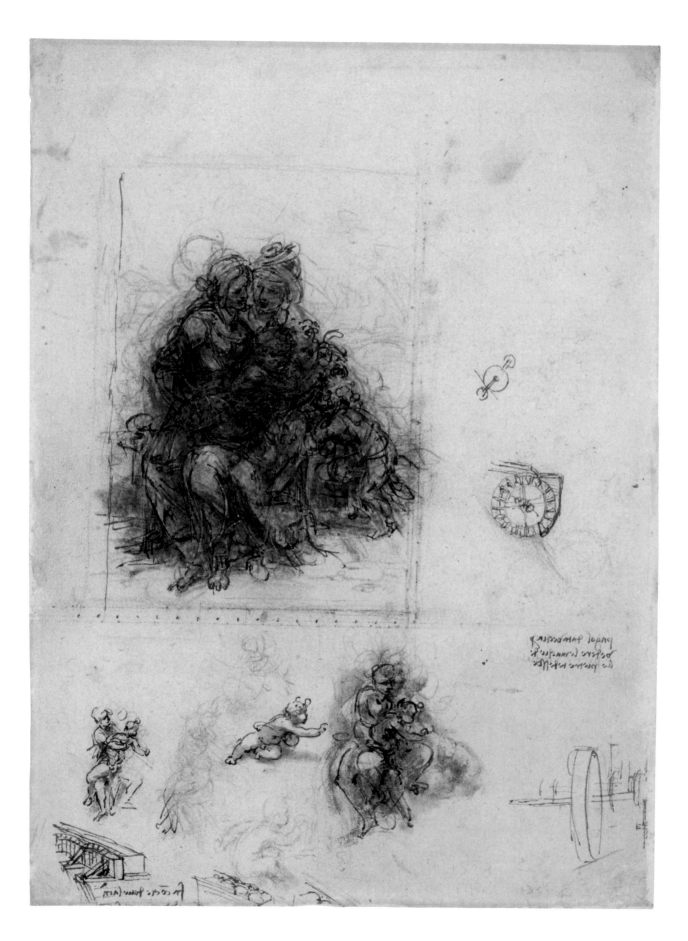

Leonardo da Vinci, *Studies for the Virgin and Child with St Anne and the Infant Baptist*, circa 1505-08, British Museum, London

Leonardo da Vinci, *Studies for the Virgin and Child with St Anne and the Infant Baptist, circa 1505-08*, British Museum, London (verso)

Richard Serra, *Remember Me Whispers the Dust*, 2001

Remember Me Whispers the Dust, 2001, (p. 22) for example, shares with Leonardo's studies a predicating faith in intuited possibilities confirmed by judgement: make the marks according to the exigencies of the moment, and accept or reject the end result. This is particularly true of Serra's works in series. 'I usually don't know which drawings have fulfilled my intention until I've made several', he explained in 2010. 'The drawings become critical of each other, and I don't judge them until I have done quite a few. That said, given the processes I use, it's easy to lose control, and it's obvious when you've made a mess, not a drawing.'[8]

That risk is heightened when there are no external criteria for assessment, whether they be the protocols of figuration, the self-imposed rules that many of Serra's early contemporaries devised, or the disorderly thematic frameworks that attend contemporary art in an era of interpretive surfeit. It starts to matter a great deal that *Remember Me Whispers the Dust* converts certain metaphors familiar from graphic conventions into immediate physical facts. The clearest example is the concept of a line having weight. In ordinary usage, that refers to the breadth of a line. Strictly speaking, and all other things being equal, a line of greater visual weight also has greater physical weight by virtue of the additional ink it requires. This is not something of which we have any reason to be conscious when the effect of a line is almost exclusively visual. The lines in *Remember Me Whispers the Dust*, as in the *Orchard Street* drawings, are primarily instances of accumulated matter, often to the point where those accumulations simultaneously obscure and emphasise the line itself. In this respect, it is not sufficient to talk of a line merely having weight. The lines *are* weight. Rather than suggesting something by analogy – shading, modelling, contours – they establish irreducibly present physical properties of their own.

A related situation arises in Serra's sense of colour. Even astute commentators can find his commitment to black counterintuitive in this regard, as Hal Foster discovered when he suggested that colour is not pronounced in Serra's work. 'It is if you think black is a colour!' Serra retorted. 'Then it's very pronounced in my work.'[9] This is, of course, an atypically constrained approach to colour, but the point is valid: gradations and effects can proliferate within a narrow spectrum, just as they do within a broad spectrum. Black is so dense that its capacity to absorb and reflect light exceeds any alternative. In *Orchard Street #85* and *#86*, for example, there is a sharp difference in light absorption or reflectance according to the localised forces that Serra imposed, and to the texture of their legacy. This kind of variation typifies Serra's transfers from the verso. Sometimes, as in the *Tracks* series, 2007-08, (p. 25) it is the dominant visual and physical effect.

Serra has asserted that 'black is a property, not a quality',[10] a distinction that John Locke addressed in terms of primary and secondary qualities.[11] This is to view black as a foundational fact – an intrinsic and predicating condition of the material and its use – rather than as a subjective effect or sensation that depends upon the way it is used.

Insofar as the distinction matters for the viewer, it is a reminder of Serra's desire to expel the aesthetic implications of artistic expressions or statements that might impede the experience of the phenomena he generates. (It is also a reminder that Serra evades the stereotypical role of 'artist as master creator'.)[12] 'I want to avoid a surface which could be read as gestural', he said of his drawings that condition interior spaces.[13] Those drawings focus the viewer's experience on the adjusted spatial situation, not on the process of fabrication or the black fields independent of the setting. The *Orchard Street* drawings do not suppress gesture in the same way, nor do they need to: they are framed drawings to be addressed directly, so that movement in relation to the drawing reveals different aspects of it. These drawings do, however, consign gesture to a structural rather than expressive role; skeleton rather than skin.

Soon after Serra began to use these techniques in his drawings, he noted that few artists – with the possible exception of Jasper Johns – suppressed the gesture while retaining the particular nature of given marks. Serra's reservations about the 'romantic gestural sign of Abstract Expressionism',[14] as he put it, were recurring doubts for artists whose idioms coalesced from the mid-1950s until the end of the 1960s, if not later. There are numerous other rhetorical motifs of advanced art from which Serra's work also distances itself, including even the least mystical readings of black fields as voids. Gesture, however, is unusually complicated in relation to a drawing practice that depends entirely on the conversion of forces from manipulated tools into direct marking on sheets of paper. Even with the verso/recto distinction, the paper is a permeable membrane rather than a neutralising barrier. In *Orchard Street #102*, for example, the recto preserves clear evidence of the force and direction of Serra's impressions. Across the series itself, the recurring arrays of vertical lines, and the differing quantities and qualities of matter they have accumulated, remain the irreducible bond that distinguishes this series from others. Gesture might be vestigial or indirect in these drawings, but it remains present.

Richard Serra, *Tracks #34*, 2007

The 'romantic gestural sign' to which Serra referred exaggerates the presence of the artist. Gestures can lend themselves to semiotic bubbles, inflated beyond reason to the point where both object and artist become fetishised ciphers; no longer truly themselves. One consequence is a general decline into ill-considered mannerism, where followers emulate results without necessarily understanding how or why those results first arose. For Serra, who has related his practices to an aphoristic summary of Giambattista Vico's argument for exact verifiability in the social sciences ('We only know what we ourselves have made'),[15] those emulations would be little more than illusions regardless of their physical reality.

The notion of 'gesture', though useful for broad categorisation of end results, is open to abuse. The techniques of Willem de Kooning, for example, are not intrinsically more gestural than those found in a seventeenth-century Dutch still life. The difference resides in the intentions. Still-life painters construct a series of gestural marks into a final result wherein the gestures are typically suppressed, or at least dissociated from the hand of the painter and made to serve the imperatives of depicted figures. The marks indicate their source, but only in isolation. As a group, they conspire to emulate an aspect of apparent reality. The gestural idioms of 1950s painting might also construct wholes, but they never shed their indexical relationship with the conditions of their making. Those that most clearly indicate the creative gesture do so because they lead to no other conclusion. Such gestures have a primacy that Serra's technique subordinates to physical accumulations, which become more prominent as Serra's gestures become more assertive, emphatic, or recapitulative. Instead of gestural expression, Serra's drawings employ gestural construction. The gestures are a means but never an end in themselves; vehicle, not destination.

One consequence of this is that Serra has developed a method in which the gestural capacity of the artist is displaced onto material that develops a gestural life of its own. Along with the structural arrays of verticals, each of the *Orchard Street* drawings contains its own pattern of matter distributed according to the physical forces that conditioned fabrication of that drawing. The slight, attenuated arcs in *#99* evince directional forces that come into play beyond Serra's drawn impressions. His drawing process generates marks independently of deliberate intention, though not of deliberate actions; incidents, not accidents. The feathered discolouration of the paper around isolated areas of ink in *#90* and *#67*, or the complex elision of heavily worked passages in *#58*, are familiar traits of graphic media. The fingerprints in *#93* are merely episodes of process no more significant than any other evidence of how the sheet of paper is handled. These kinds of incidents might be treated as clues, if one so wishes, but they cannot be treated as part of a code. There is plenty to understand but nothing to decipher.

If the choice of drawings in the *Orchard Street* series has an organising principle, perhaps it is best understood as a contemporary echo of the Renaissance idea of *dimostrazione*: the display of ingenuity and problem-solving. There is no narrative, but there is unquestionably an ethos that becomes apparent over time. This is related to Serra's observation that, when he works in series, 'the drawings become critical of each other'. One key difference is that Serra is concerned with the present tense – imperfect, heuristic, an open situation in which things happen – rather than with a quest for perfected closure. 'Drawing is a tightly bound convention and there are very few avenues out of it', he said in 1992.[16] If there is no clear way out, the most promising alternative is to keep moving.

When drawing is stripped of narrative, translated imagery, environmental modification or even the appeal to connoisseurship that conventional handling might permit, we are largely abandoned by the comfortable habits that attend the medium. We, too, have few avenues out of the tightly bound convention that Serra encounters as a practitioner. Possibly we flee too readily from discussing experiences that do not lend themselves to general rules or common ground, even though the kinds of experiences that Serra's works prompt in the viewer are necessarily idiomatic. In some cases, the viewer is both activated and activating. *Delineator*, 1974-75, (p. 29) for example, invites the viewer to stand on the steel plate on the floor and gaze up at a transverse-mounted plate on the ceiling. The viewer becomes the crucial reconciling element that completes the work, allows it to make sense. This physical role is difficult to assimilate into a body of convention that confers primacy on the eye. Rejection of interceding frameworks that seek explanation or description, however, implies a shift away from visualisation as an exercise in deciphering – the search for legibility, for something to read and put into words – and towards the more immediate and intimate sense of touch.

The sensuous aspects of Serra's work, which have caught the attention of commentators in recent years,[17] are all the more poignant amid the crisis of proximity that has conditioned our expectations regarding physical relations under restrictive public-health measures. Tactile gratification as an aesthetic experience has always been present in Serra's practices, even if the formidable body of commentary surrounding them has focused on austere themes that are merely part of the whole. Serra acknowledges this aspect of his sculptures, although it is an incidental aspect of his intentions: 'I do talk about the surfaces as skins. I think people have largely lost their sense of touch, and if my work reactivates that need or desire, that's fine with me. I can't deny that people like to touch the work.'[18]

Richard Serra, *Delineator*, 1974-75, The Museum of Modern Art, New York

Insofar as Serra's ethos is phenomenological – with a set of values inextricable from the experiences of living human beings in real time – it contains at least the promise of universal validity. Symbolic systems, metaphysical allegories, and of course visual illusions, all play central roles in artistic expression. These are things we can learn to interpret. They are not, however, things we can touch. As any artisan, parent or lover is quick to grasp, there is no substitute for the self-contained reality of tactile engagement. A drawing that generates its own tactility contains the promise of unique immediacy. We take that state for granted as we pass through the world but seldom expect it from graphic conventions. Those of us who have endured the substitution of images for real presence in human relations might find in Serra's drawings an unusually cogent argument for the most tangible of experiences, even where we least expect them.

1   Gary Garrels, 'An Interview With Richard Serra' (2010), in Gary Garrels, Bernice Rose, and Michelle White, eds., *Richard Serra Drawing: A Retrospective*, exh. cat., Houston: Menil Collection, 2011, p. 65; and Richard Serra and Hal Foster, *Conversations About Sculpture*, New Haven and London: Yale University Press, 2018, p. 7.

2   Serra, interviewed by Nicholas Serota and David Sylvester, 'Interview' (1992), in *Richard Serra, Writings/Interviews*, Chicago and London: University of Chicago Press, 1994, p. 279.

3   Serra and Foster, *Conversations about Sculpture*, p. 34.

4   George Kubler, *The Shape of Time: Remarks on the History of Things*, New Haven and London: Yale University Press, 1962, p. 74.

5   Serra and Foster, *Conversations about Sculpture*, p. 198.

6   Giorgio Vasari, *Lives of the Painters, Sculptors and Architects* (1568), v. 1, trans. Gaston du C. de Vere, London: Everyman's Library, 1996, p. 103.

7   Ernst Gombrich, *Gombrich on the Renaissance*, v. 1, *Norm and Form*, London: Phaidon, 1966, p. 58.

8   Serra, in Garrels, 'An Interview With Richard Serra', p. 83.

9   Serra and Foster, *Conversations about Sculpture*, p. 12.

10   Serra, 'Notes on Drawing' (1987), in *Writings, Interviews*, p. 179.

11   John Locke, *An Essay Concerning Human Understanding* (1689), Book II, Chapter VIII, § 8-10.

12   Clara Weyergraf-Serra, in Serra and Foster, *Conversations about Sculpture*, p. 255.

13   Serra, interviewed by Lynne Cooke, 'Interview' (1992), in *Writings, Interviews*, p. 254.

14   Ibid., p. 259.

15   Serra, statement in *Richard Serra: Line Drawings*, exh. cat., New York: Gagosian, 2002, p. 7.

16   Serra, interviewed by Lynne Cooke, 'Interview', p. 258.

17   See, for example, Neil Cox, 'The Shape of Feeling', in *Richard Serra: Drawings 2015-2017*, exh. cat., New York: Gagosian and Göttingen: Steidl, 2017, pp. 11-21; and Gordon Hughes, 'Over/Drawing/Drawing/Over', in *Richard Serra: Vertical and Horizontal Reversals*, exh. cat., New York: David Zwirner and Göttingen: Steidl, 2015, pp. 6-17. Tactile disengagement was also a theme in the author's lecture at Kunsthaus Bregenz, Austria, in June 2008, which had its roots in several conversations with Serra earlier that year.

18   Serra and Foster, *Conversations about Sculpture*, p. 122.

I think my whole drawing practice is involved with repetition, knowing there's no possibility of repeating, knowing that it's going to yield something different every time.

—RICHARD SERRA

THE WORKS

RICHARD SERRA (B. 1938)   *Orchard Street #58*, 2018

RICHARD SERRA (B. 1938)   *Orchard Street #67*, 2018

RICHARD SERRA (B. 1938)   *Orchard Street #68*, 2018

RICHARD SERRA (B. 1938)   *Orchard Street #69*, 2018

RICHARD SERRA (B. 1938)   *Orchard Street #71*, 2018

RICHARD SERRA (B. 1938)   *Orchard Street #72, 2018*

RICHARD SERRA (B. 1938) *Orchard Street #75, 2018*

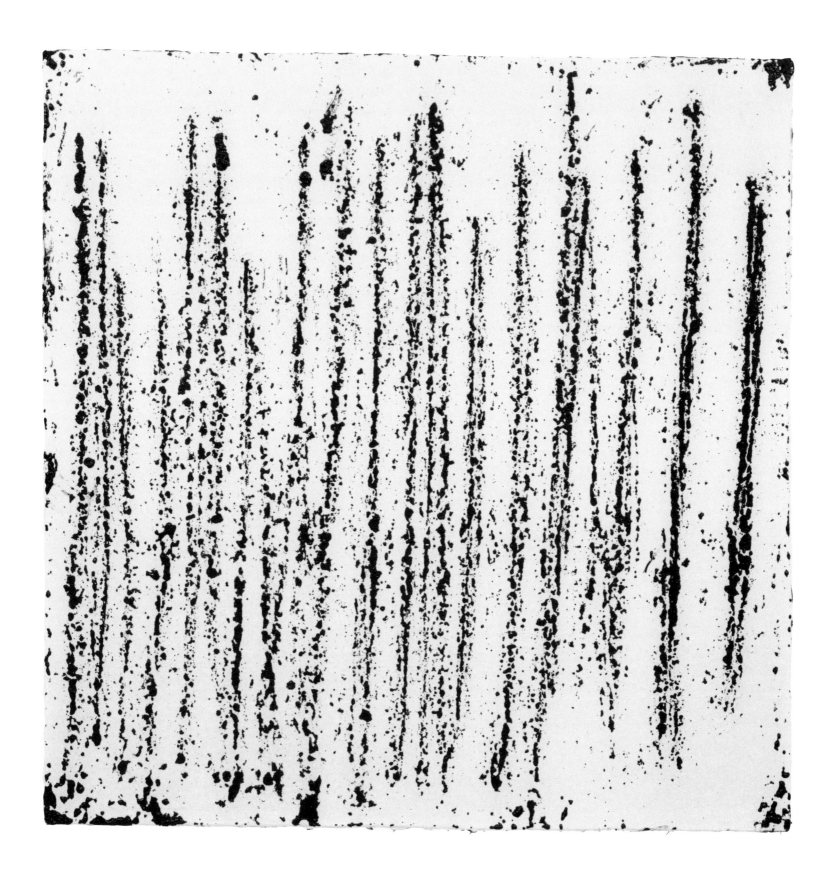

RICHARD SERRA (B. 1938)   *Orchard Street #82, 2018*

RICHARD SERRA (B. 1938)   *Orchard Street #84*, 2018

RICHARD SERRA (B. 1938)   *Orchard Street #85*, 2018

RICHARD SERRA (B. 1938)   *Orchard Street #86*, 2018

RICHARD SERRA (B. 1938)   *Orchard Street #87, 2018*

RICHARD SERRA (B. 1938)   *Orchard Street #90*, 2018

RICHARD SERRA (B. 1938)   *Orchard Street #91*, 2018

RICHARD SERRA (B. 1938)   *Orchard Street #93, 2018*

RICHARD SERRA (B. 1938) *Orchard Street #96, 2018*

RICHARD SERRA (B. 1938)   *Orchard Street #98*, 2018

RICHARD SERRA (B. 1938)   *Orchard Street #99, 2018*

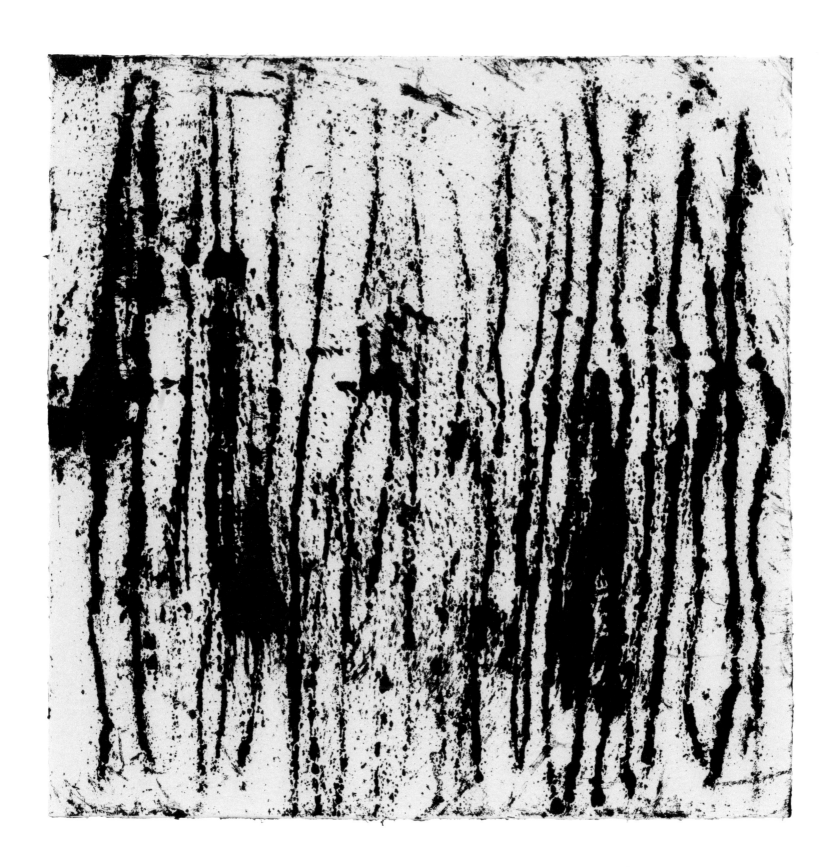

RICHARD SERRA (B. 1938)   *Orchard Street #102*, 2018

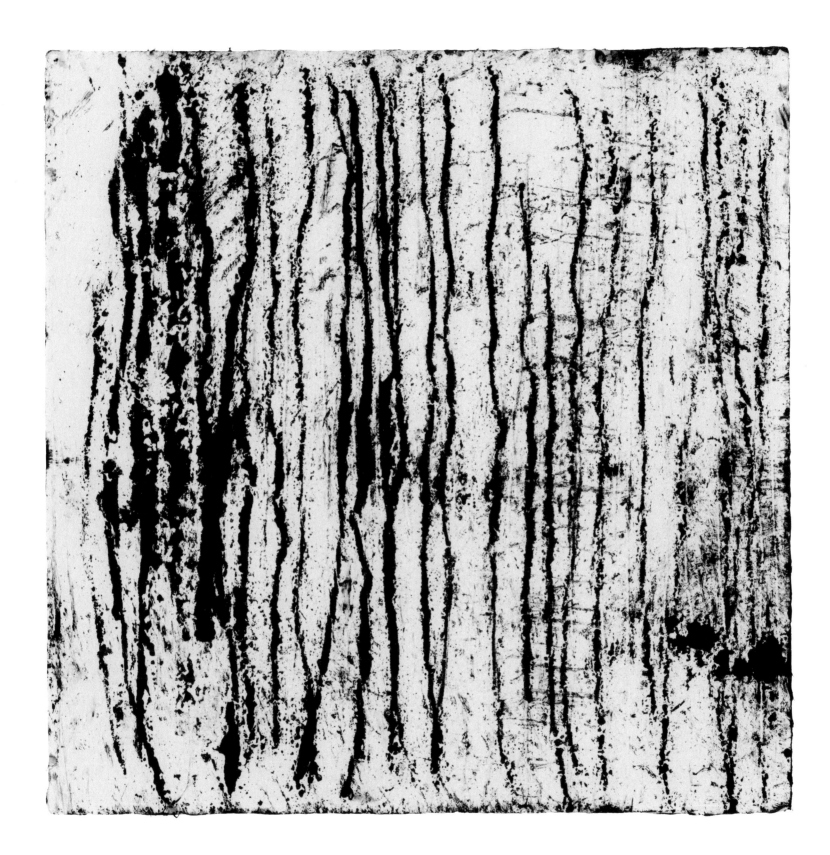

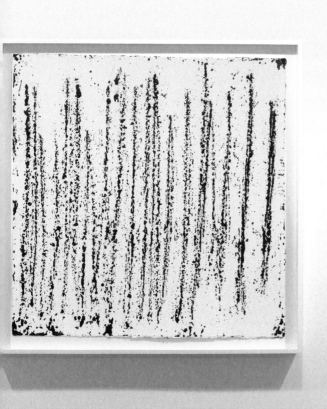

34—35

Orchard Street #58
etching ink and silica
on handmade paper
40 $^1/_2$ × 40 $^1/_4$ in. (102.9 × 102.2 cm.)
Executed in 2018

36—37

Orchard Street #67
etching ink and silica
on handmade paper
39 ³/₄ × 39 ³/₄ in. (101 × 101 cm.)
Executed in 2018

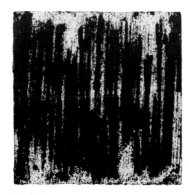

38—39

Orchard Street #68
etching ink and silica
on handmade paper
39 ³/₄ × 40 in. (101 × 101.6 cm.)
Executed in 2018

40—41

Orchard Street #69
etching ink and silica
on handmade paper
39 × 39 in. (99.1 × 99.1 cm.)
Executed in 2018

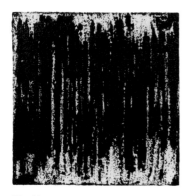

42—43

Orchard Street #71
etching ink and silica
on handmade paper
39 × 39 in. (99.1 × 99.1 cm.)
Executed in 2018

44—45

Orchard Street #72
etching ink and silica
on handmade paper
39 ³/₄ × 40 in. (101 × 101.6 cm.)
Executed in 2018

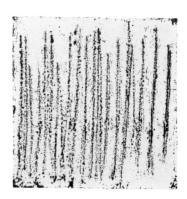

46—47

Orchard Street #75
etching ink and silica
on handmade paper
39 ¹/₄ × 39 in. (99.7 × 99.1 cm.)
Executed in 2018

48—49

Orchard Street #82
etching ink and silica
on handmade paper
40 $^1/_4$ × 40 $^1/_2$ in. (102.2 × 102.9 cm.)
Executed in 2018

50—51

Orchard Street #84
etching ink and silica
on handmade paper
40 × 40 $^1/_4$ in. (101.6 × 102.2 cm.)
Executed in 2018

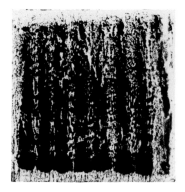

52—53

Orchard Street #85
etching ink and silica
on handmade paper
40 $^1/_4$ × 39 $^3/_4$ in. (102.2 × 101 cm.)
Executed in 2018

54—55

Orchard Street #86
etching ink and silica
on handmade paper
40 $^1/_4$ × 40 $^1/_4$ in. (102.2 × 102.2 cm.)
Executed in 2018

56—57

Orchard Street #87
etching ink and silica
on handmade paper
47 $^1/_4$ × 31 $^1/_2$ in. (120 × 80 cm.)
Executed in 2018

58—59

Orchard Street #90
etching ink and silica
on handmade paper
40 × 40 in. (101.6 × 101.6 cm.)
Executed in 2018

60—61

Orchard Street #91
etching ink and silica
on handmade paper
47 ¹/₄ × 31 ¹/₂ in. (120 × 80 cm.)
Executed in 2018

62—63

Orchard Street #93
etching ink and silica
on handmade paper
47 × 31 ¹/₂ in. (119.4 × 80 cm.)
Executed in 2018

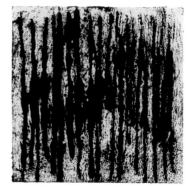

64—65

Orchard Street #96
etching ink and silica
on handmade paper
39 × 39 ¹/₄ in. (99.1 × 99.7 cm.)
Executed in 2018

66—67

Orchard Street #98
etching ink and silica
on handmade paper
39 × 39 ¹/₄ in. (99.1 × 99.7 cm.)
Executed in 2018

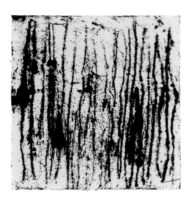

68—69

Orchard Street #99
etching ink and silica
on handmade paper
39 × 39 in. (99.1 × 99.1 cm.)
Executed in 2018

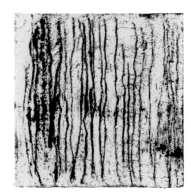

70—71

Orchard Street #102
etching ink and silica
on handmade paper
39 × 39 ¹/₄ in. (99.1 × 99.7 cm.)
Executed in 2018

Published on the occasion of the exhibition
Richard Serra Drawings
16 September – 17 December 2021

ORDOVAS
25 SAVILE ROW LONDON W1S 2ER
T +44 (0)20 7287 5013
WWW.ORDOVASART.COM

Publication © 2021 Ordovas
Introduction © Pilar Ordovas
Accumulated Experience © James Lawrence

Editor: Pilar Ordovas
Project managers: Georgina Rumbellow, Silvia Ricci and Natasha Rosenblatt
Copy editor: Liane Jones

Design by Sinéad Madden
Printed in England by Pureprint, Uckfield

ISBN 978-1-9996681-8-1

Photography: page 5: Photograph by Gianfranco Gorgoni
© Maya Gorgoni; pages 20 and 21: © The Trustees of the British Museum;
pages 35, 37, 39, 41, 43, 45, 47, 49, 51, 53, 55, 57, 59, 61, 63, 65, 67,
69, 71, 84, 85, 86 and 87: Photography by Robert McKeever;
pages 72, 73, 74, 75, 76, 77, 78, 79, 80, 81 and 82: Photography by Andrew Smart.

We would like to extend our profound thanks to
Allen Glatter, James Lawrence, Robert McKeever, Trina McKeever,
John Silberman and Clara Weyergraf-Serra
for all their time and willingness to help, as well as for their
important contributions to this exhibition.

A special thanks to Richard Serra.